MACHINES AT WORK

Motorbikes

Clive Gifford

WAYLAND

Published in 2013 by Wayland
Copyright © Wayland 2013

Wayland
338 Euston Road
London NW1 3BH

Wayland Australia
Level 17/207 Kent Street
Sydney, NSW 2000

Editor: Nicola Edwards
Designer: Elaine Wilkinson
Picture Researcher: Clive Gifford

British Library Cataloguing in Publication
Data

Gifford, Clive.
    Motorbikes. -- (Machines at work)
    1. Motorcycles--Juvenile literature.
    I. Title II. Series
    629.2'275-dc23

ISBN: 978 0 7502 7805 8

10 9 8 7 6 5 4 3 2 1

Printed in China

Wayland is a division of Hachette Children's
Books, an Hachette UK company
www.hachette.co.uk

To find out about the author, visit his website:
www.clivegifford.co.uk

Picture acknowledgements: The author
and publisher would like to thank the
following for allowing their pictures to
be reproduced in this publication: Cover
(main) Julie Lucht / Shutterstock.com,
(inset) asiana / Shutterstock.com; title page
Stephen Mcsweeny / Shutterstock.com;
pp2-3 taelove7 / Shutterstock.com; p4
Getty Images; p5 (t) Shutterstock © Lola, (b)
7382489561 / Shutterstock.com; p6 Mark
Yuill / Shutterstock.com; p7 (t) Shutterstock
© Katrina Brown, (b) Shutterstock ©
Jordache; p8 taelove7 / Shutterstock.com; p9
(t) iStock © Damir Spanic, (b) Tupungato /
Shutterstock.com; p10 (t) Stephen Mcsweeny
/ Shutterstock.com, (b) Red_hayabusa /
Shutterstock.com; p11 Giovanna Tondelli
/ Shutterstock.com; p12 Getty Images;
p13 (t) Shutterstock © azaphoto, (b) Alvin
Ganesh / Shutterstock.com; p14 mobil11 /
Shutterstock.com; p15 (t) iStock © graham
heywood, (b) iStock © 4X-image; p16
Pospisil MRL / Shutterstock.com; p17 (t)
DSPA / Shutterstock.com, (b) KuuLeeR /
Shutterstock.com; p18 Graham Prentice /
Shutterstock.com; p19 Shutterstock © risteski
goce; p20 Jordan Tan / Shutterstock.com;
p21 (t) Thomas Bedenk / Shutterstock.com,
(b) jan kranendonk / Shutterstock.com; p22
(t) Pospisil MRL / Shutterstock.com, (b)
Mark Yuill / Shutterstock.com; p23 mobil11
/ Shutterstock.com; p24 Pospisil MRL /
Shutterstock.com

Contents

Motorbikes on the move

Motorbikes are vehicles that run on two wheels. An engine burns fuel and provides the power that turns the motorbike's wheels. As the wheels turn, the motorbike travels forward. Many motorbikes are used for work but some are ridden for fun or to compete in races.

Rider grips handlebars

FAST FACT

There are over 200 million motorbikes in use. Over half of these are in Asia.

Front wheel covered in a rubber tyre

ZOOM IN

Most motorcycles are driven by a chain, a lot like the one on your bicycle. The engine pulls on the chain which then turns the motorbike's back wheel round.

Motorbikes are used all over the world as a cheap form of transport. Most cost much less to build and run than cars. They can be used to deliver items quickly to customers. Motorbikes can be fitted with different racks and attachments to carry things.

Rider sits on saddle

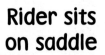

This powerful machine races on tracks, at speeds of over 300km/h.

Engine underneath this body part, called a fairing

A motorbike rider delivers farm produce in India.

Engine power

A motorbike engine burns fuel. The burning fuel creates gases which move parts inside the engine. Most motorbikes have smaller engines than cars. As they are smaller and lighter in weight, they don't need as much engine power to move.

The engine is cooled by air travelling past it.

Exhaust pipe

FAST FACT

The Triumph Rocket III's motorcycle engine is a monster! It is almost twice the size of engines used in many small cars.

Chain turns the rear wheel

Fuel tank stores liquid fuel

ZOOM IN

Burning fuel creates waste gases. Metal tubes called exhaust pipes carry these gases away from the engine and out behind the motorbike.

Most motorbikes are started by the rider turning a key to fire up the engine. To start some older motorbikes riders have to press a foot pedal down sharply. This is called a kick start.

Rubber tyres grip the road

To start this motorbike, the rider turns an ignition key.

Steering

A rider steers a motorbike using handlebars in a similar way to riding a bicycle. When riders want to steer round a bend or corner, they turn the handlebars. The front wheel turns and the rest of the bike follows in the same direction.

Turning a sharp corner, these racers lean their bikes into the bend. They will move back into an upright position as they complete their turn.

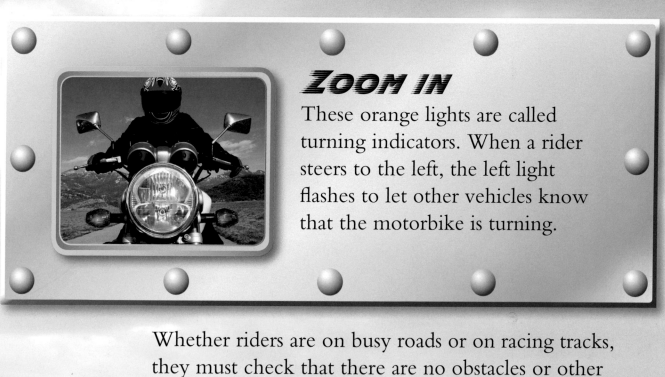

ZOOM IN

These orange lights are called turning indicators. When a rider steers to the left, the left light flashes to let other vehicles know that the motorbike is turning.

Whether riders are on busy roads or on racing tracks, they must check that there are no obstacles or other vehicles in their way before they make a turn.

Motorbikes can turn easily to weave in and out of busy city traffic. This allows couriers to deliver packages speedily and other motorcyclists to get to work quickly.

Speeding up

The righthand grip on a motorbike's handlebars is called the throttle. When a rider twists the throttle, the engine works harder and sends more power to the rear wheel. This makes the motorbike go faster.

This is called a wheelie. The rider increases the engine power sharply. The rear wheel thrusts forward and the front wheel lifts off the ground.

ZOOM IN

This dial is called a speedometer. It tells a rider how fast the motorbike is going. Riders sometimes have to slow down so that they do not break the speed limit on a road.

Motorbikes at work often have to travel fast. Couriers sometimes have to speed up and change road lanes to overtake slower vehicles. Police motorcyclists may have to go even faster to catch speeding cars or to race to the scene of a crime.

FAST FACT

The Suzuki Hayabusa motorcycle can speed up faster than most other bikes. It can move from a standstill to 100km/h in under 3 seconds.

An Italian police motorcyclist speeds through town to answer an emergency call.

Riding safely

Motorbike riders do not have the frame of a car around them to protect them if they crash. So they have to wear plenty of special clothing and keep their machine under control at all times.

Crash helmet cushions and protects head

Padded leather gloves protect hands

This rider has crashed and been thrown clear of his motorbike. He was protected by his safety clothing and walked away unharmed.

Motorcycle boots have steel toecaps

Pads on knees are called knee sliders

Motorbike riders try to stay safe by using their brakes to slow down or stop to avoid a bump or crash. To make the brakes work, riders press levers which are fitted on the handlebars.

FAST FACT

The Honda Gold Wing motorbike was the first to be fitted with an airbag (a bag which blows up like a balloon if there is a crash).

ZOOM IN

The brake disc is attached to the motorbike wheel. When the brakes are used, pads press against the disc. This creates a force called friction which slows the motorbike wheel down.

Riders have used their brakes to stop at this busy road junction in Vietnam.

Off-road riding

Many motorcycles are used to travel off-road and over rough, bumpy, sandy or muddy ground. They are useful because they are able to reach places other vehicles cannot. Some, for example, are used to rescue injured walkers or climbers on hills.

Rider wears a full-face helmet

Mudguard stops dirt from the spinning front wheel hitting the rider

This off-road racing motorbike has a strong frame that can withstand a heavy landing after a jump.

Long saddle where the rider sits

Race number

Many off-road motorbikes are raced in motocross competitions. These are exciting races for as many as 40 bikes around laps of a short dirt and mud course with bumps and jumps.

Two motocross riders race side by side over a dirt course.

ZOOM IN

This spring and tube help to absorb some of the bumps felt by a rider when a motorbike lands after a jump or travels over rough ground.

Motorbike racing

Some motorbikes are raced on twisting and turning tracks that are covered with a smooth surface like a road. The fastest of all track motorbikes are MotoGP bikes. These machines are built just for racing.

Top racer Valentino Rossi rides his MotoGP motorbike. Rossi hunches low, creating a streamlined shape. This makes the bike go faster.

Powerful engine generates high speeds

Large smooth rubber tyres grip the track

ZOOM IN

MotoGP bikes are fitted with a covering at the front called a fairing. The fairing helps to smooth the flow of air around the bike, increasing its speed.

Speedway races take place on short, oval-shaped dirt tracks. Four riders take part in each race. Riders slide their motorbikes sideways into corners. They speed up to 110km/h on the straight parts of the track.

Two speedway riders race. They control their speed only using the throttle. The machines have no brakes!

Carrying loads

As well as carrying their riders and sometimes passengers, motorbikes can be used to carry other objects. Racks bolted on to the frame allow boxes and bags to be attached. This means riders can carry and deliver a variety of loads from pizzas to medical supplies.

Windshield

This motorcycle is designed for travelling long distances. It is large, has a comfortable saddle and riding position and plenty of places to store things.

ZOOM IN

A pannier is a bag or solid box that sits over the rear wheel and can be filled with the things riders need to carry with them.

Padded cushion supports the back of the rider

Top box is bolted on to the back of bike

Pannier stores spare clothing and supplies

Some motorbikes are converted into three-wheeled vehicles. The extra wheel at the back gives a stable base for carrying bigger loads.

A motorcycle sidecar is a pod containing a seat for an extra passenger. The sidecar is supported by its own wheel. This helps to keep the motorcycle balanced.

Emergency bikes

Motorbikes are used by emergency services to reach fires, accidents and crime scenes more quickly than cars and trucks. They can travel fast down narrow streets and are easy to stop and park. The rider can get off the bike quickly to look after an injured person or chase a suspect on foot.

Police motorcycles can cruise at slow speeds when they are on patrol. Here, a group of police officers on motorbikes set off on traffic patrol in Singapore.

Bright headlight for riding at night

Storage boxes hold tools and first aid kit

ZOOM IN

These police motorbikes have a large flashing light at the back to warn other motorists they are there. The light is switched on and off by a button on the handlebars.

A motorbike carries a battery that powers its lights and other electrical devices. Emergency motorbikes may have a second battery to power extra lights, sound speakers and other equipment.

Motorbike ambulances race paramedics with emergency medical supplies to the scene of an accident.

FAST FACT

Fire-fighters are testing out special fire bikes. The motorbikes are fitted with their own tanks of water and a 30m-long hose.

Quiz

How much have you found out about motorbikes at work? Try this quick quiz!

1. Which continent is home to over half of all the world's motorbikes?
a) Europe
b) Asia
c) North America

2. Which control does the rider use to change the speed of the motorbike?
a) Throttle
b) Ignition
c) Brakes

3. MotoGP bikes are raced on what sort of course?
a) A dirt oval
b) Over cross country
c) On smooth tracks

4. What part of a motorbike uses friction between parts to slow a motorbike down?
a) Brakes
b) Steering
c) Throttle

5. Which type of motorbike has no brakes and is raced on dirt tracks?
a) MotoGP
b) Speedway
c) Motocross

6. Where would you find knee sliders?
a) In the motorbike's engine
b) On the motorbike's handlebars
c) As part of a rider's racing clothing

7. Which motorbike was the first to have an airbag fitted?
a) The Honda Gold Wing
b) The Suzuki Hayabusa
c) The Honda Super Cub

8. The Susuki Hayabusa can move from a standstill to 100 km/h in under how long?
a) one second
b) two seconds
c) three seconds

Answers: 1.b, 2.a, 3.c, 4.a, 5.b, 6.c, 7.a, 8.c

Glossary

battery a store of chemicals in a case which powers the electrical parts of a motorbike

brake lever a control on a motorbike's handlebars which operates the vehicle's brakes

crash helmet a protective hat worn by motorbike riders to stop head injuries if they fall or have a crash

exhaust pipes metal tubes which channel waste gases away from a motorbike's engine

fairing a covering at the front of a motorbike which protects the rider from wind and helps make the motorbike more streamlined

friction the force that slows movement between two objects which rub together

fuel petrol, diesel or another substance burned in an engine to make the motorbike go

fuel tank a container, usually made of metal, which holds the motorbike's fuel

motocross motorcycle races around laps of a bumpy dirt course

panniers storage containers that rest on either side of the rear wheel

saddle the padded seat of a motorbike where the rider, and sometimes a passenger will sit

siren a device which makes a loud sound on police motorcycles to warn other vehicles

speedometer a dial or electronic screen that displays a motorbike's speed

streamlined describes something that is shaped so that air travels easily and smoothly over or around it

throttle the control on the handlebars of a motorbike that changes the speed of the engine

Further Information

Books

On The Go: Motorcycles in Action, David and Penny Glover, Wayland, 2008
Machines Inside Out: Motorcycles, Chris Oxlade, Wayland, 2010
Go Turbo: Hot Bikes, Roland Brown, Franklin Watts, 2009
Extreme Machines: Motorbikes, Chris Oxlade, Franklin Watts, 2009

Websites

http://motorcycles.about.com/od/motorcyclingbasic1/a/BikeTypes.htm
Learn about different types of motorbike at this webpage.
http://www.motogp.com/
The official website of the MotoGP competition for the fastest track motorbikes.

Places To Visit

The National Motorcycle Museum, Coventry Road, Solihull, West Midlands B92 0EJ
http://www.nationalmotorcyclemuseum.co.uk/
This huge museum is home to more than 850 motorbikes.

The London Motorcycle Museum, Oldfield Lane South, Greenford, Middlesex UB6 9LD
http://www.london-motorcycle-museum.org/
A museum with over 100 motorbikes on display, from makers such as Harley Davidson and Triumph.

Sammy Miller Museum, Bashley Cross Roads, New Milton, Hampshire, BH25 5SZ
http://www.sammymiller.co.uk/default.asp
At this museum you can see 400 motorbikes, including rare models from history and racing.